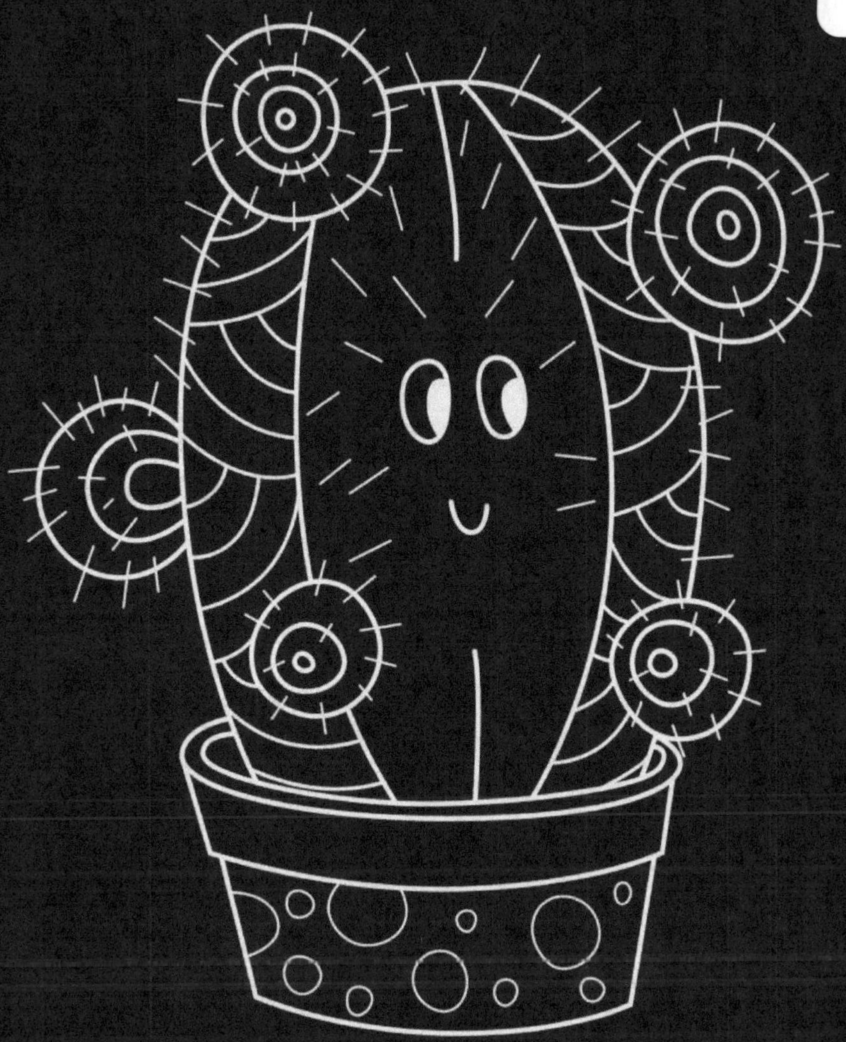

TINY CACTUS PUBLISHING

CLORIST NAME

TEST PAGE

PREPARE YOUR COLOR

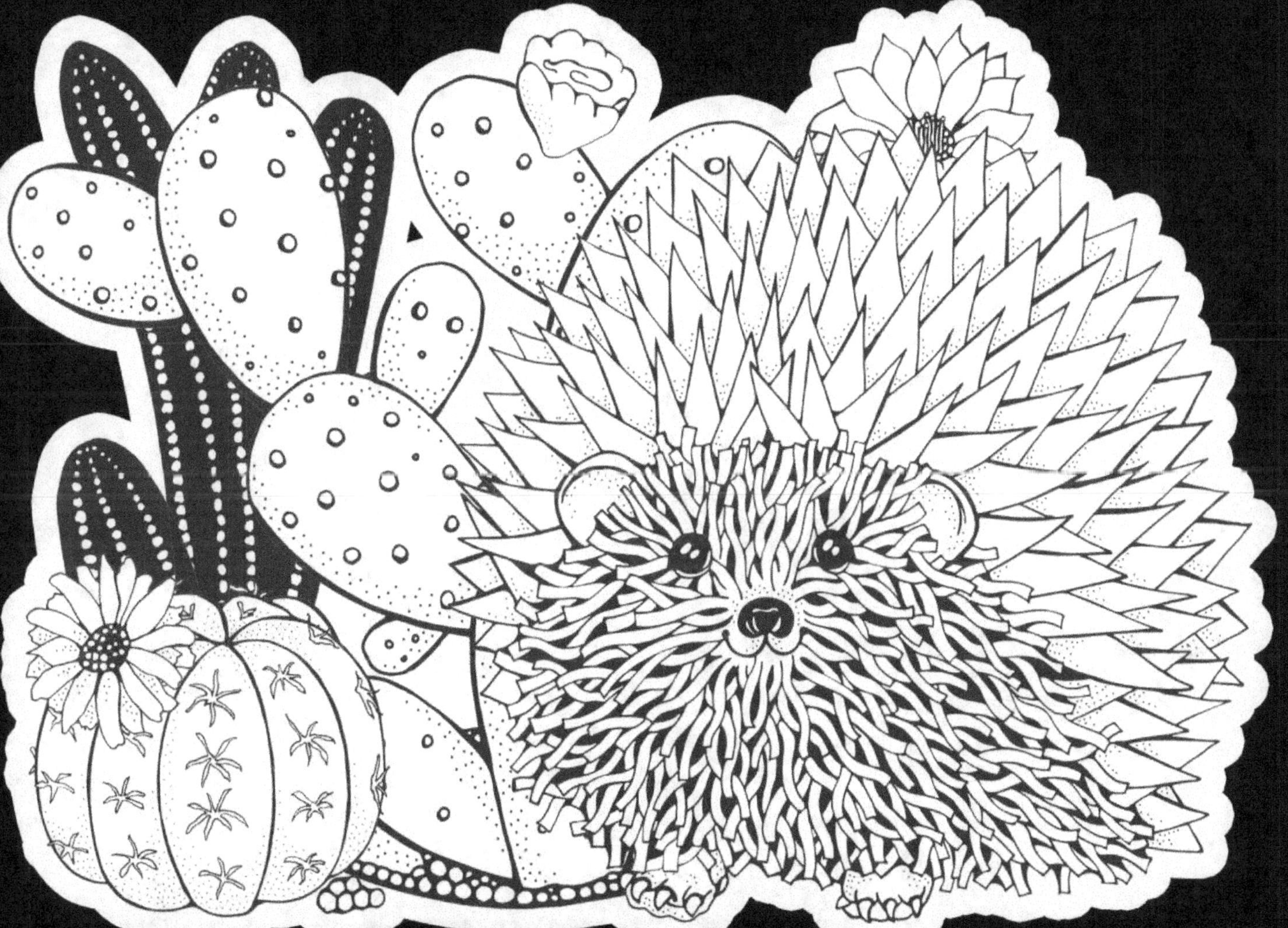

WARM UP !!

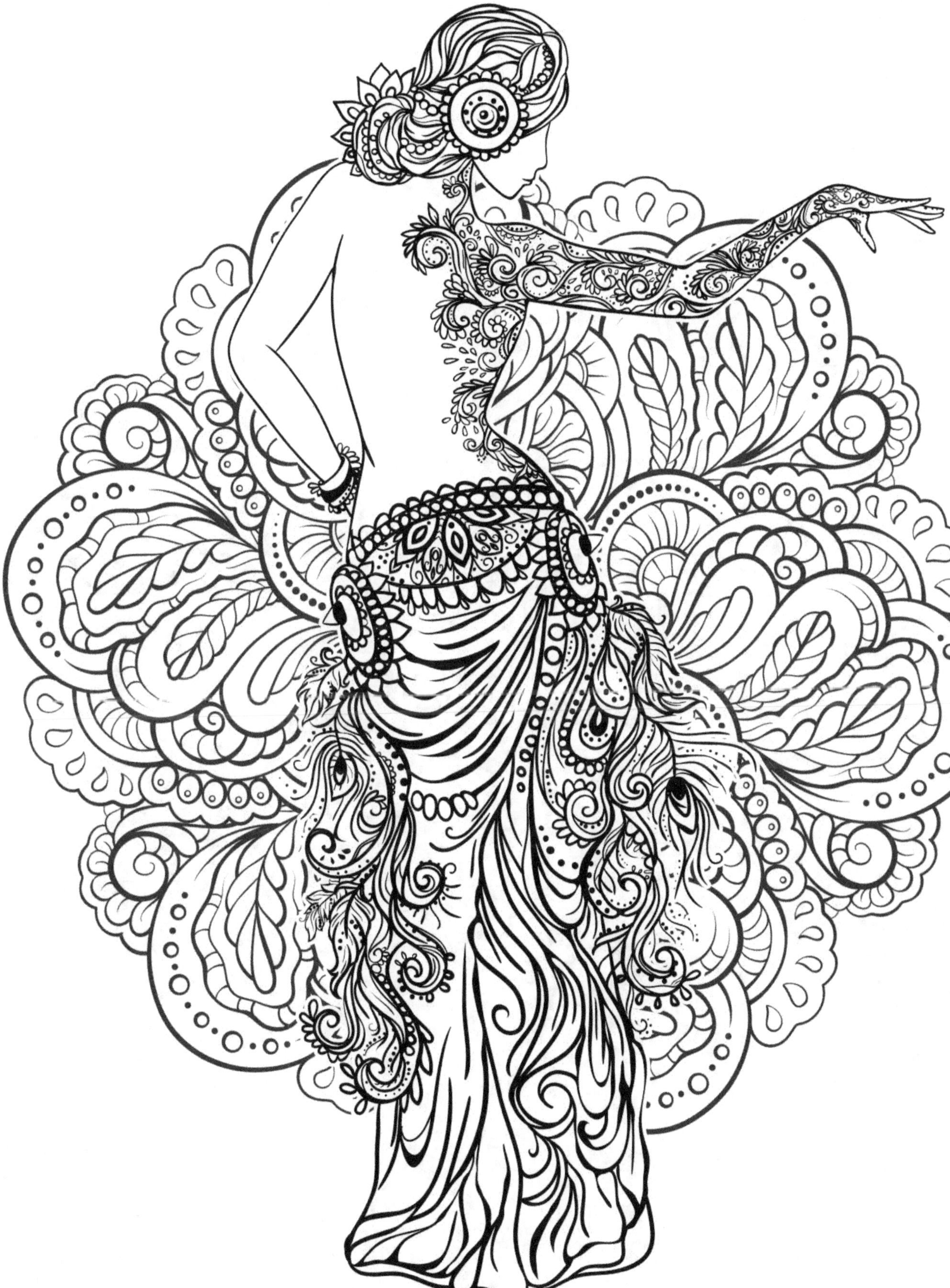

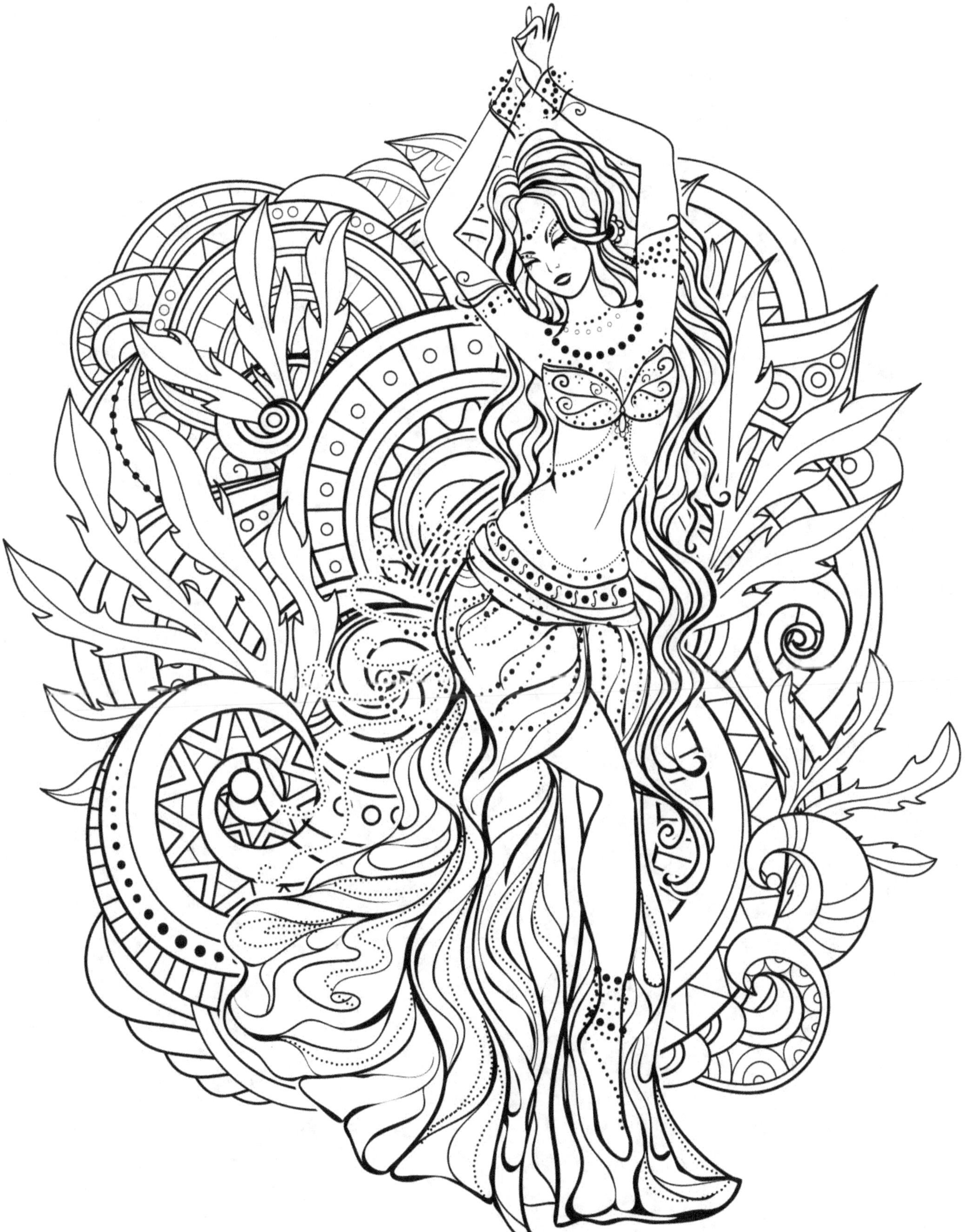

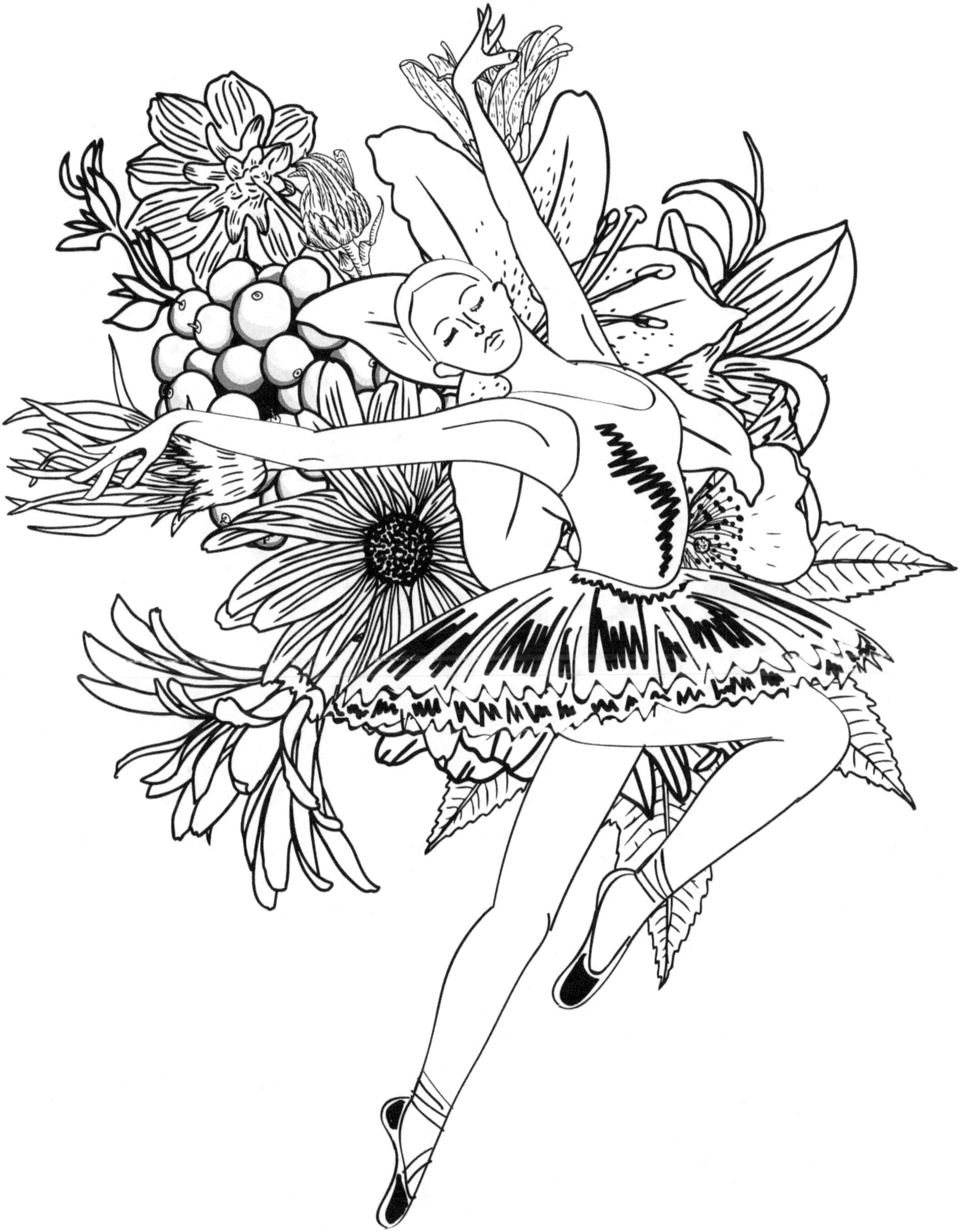

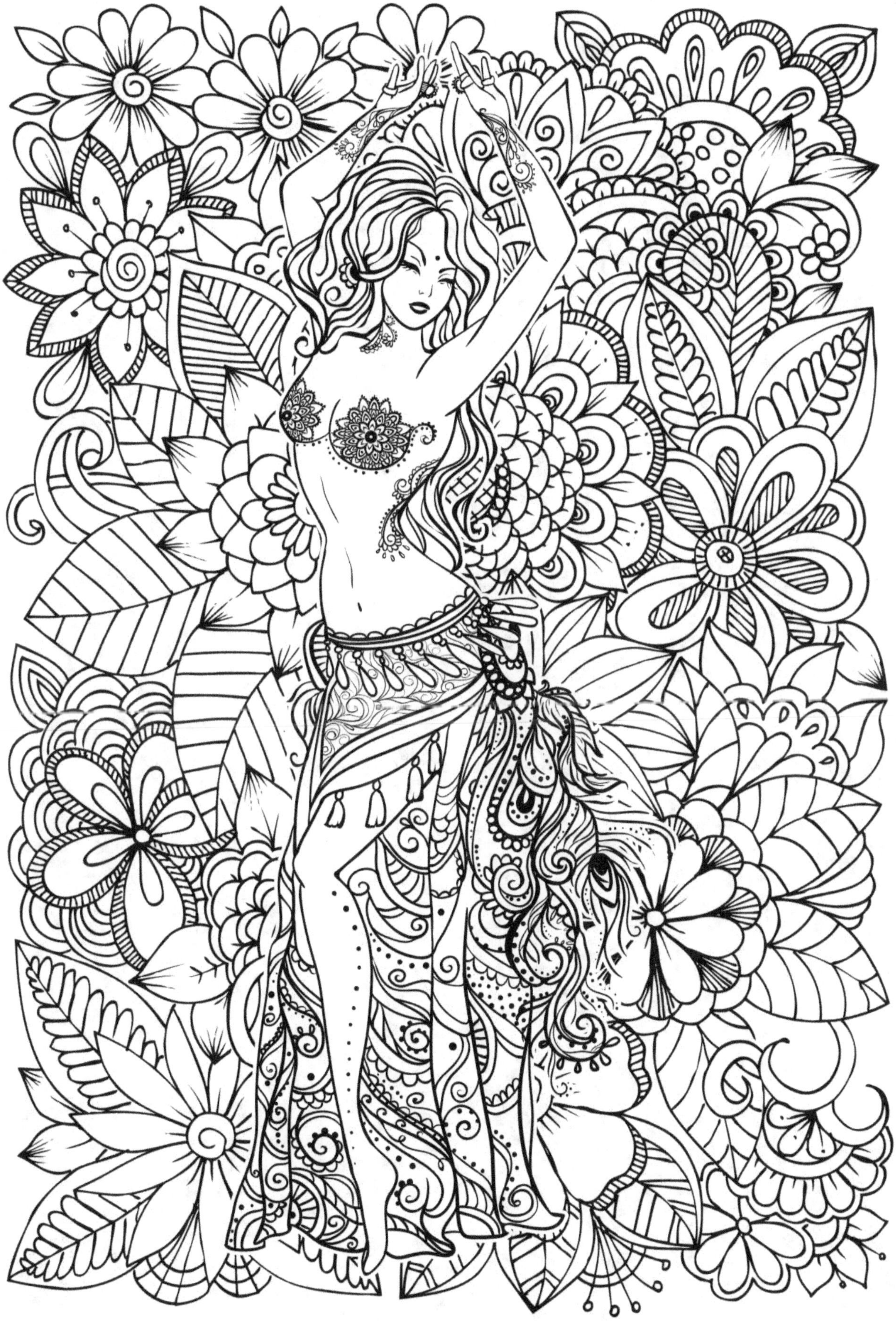

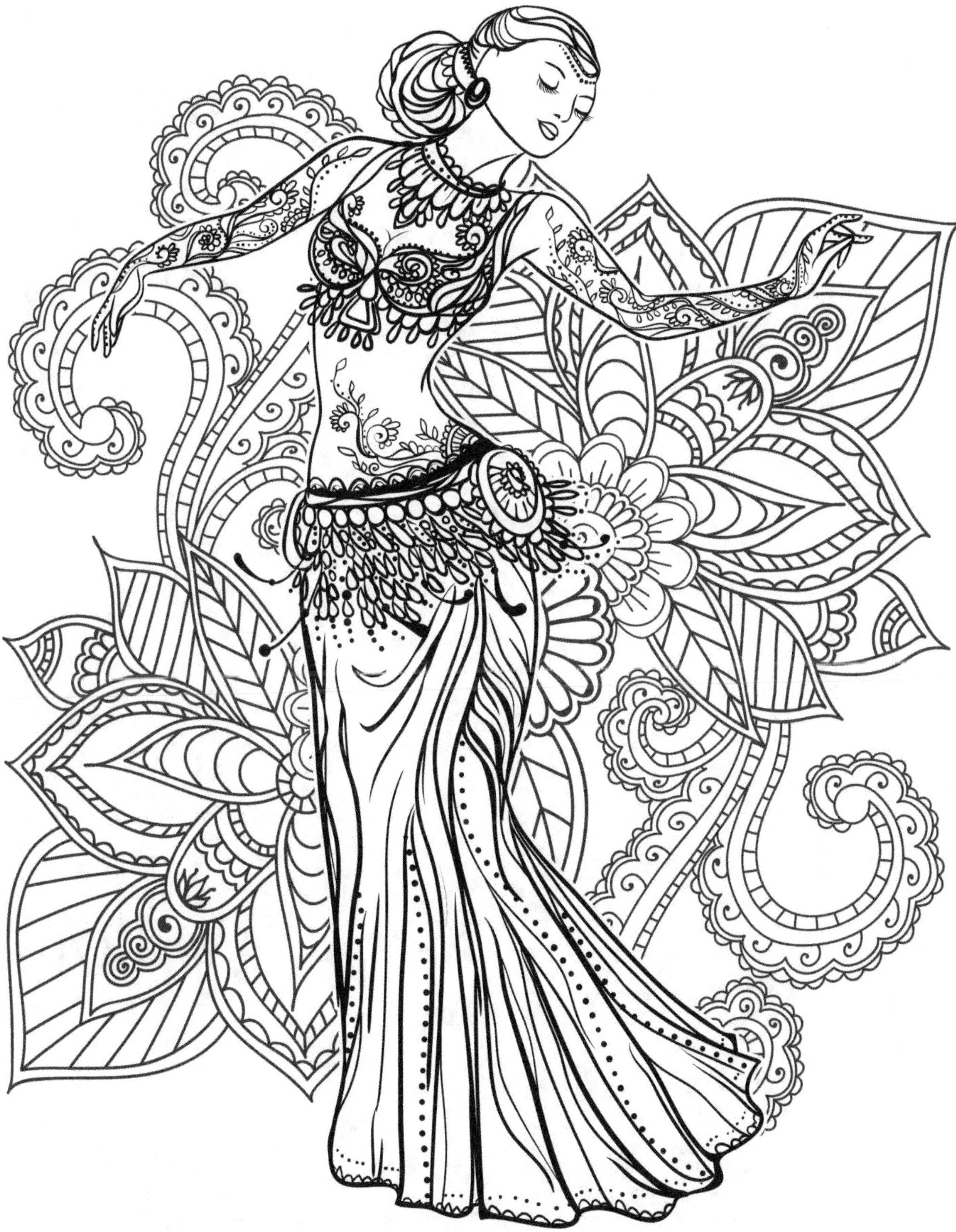

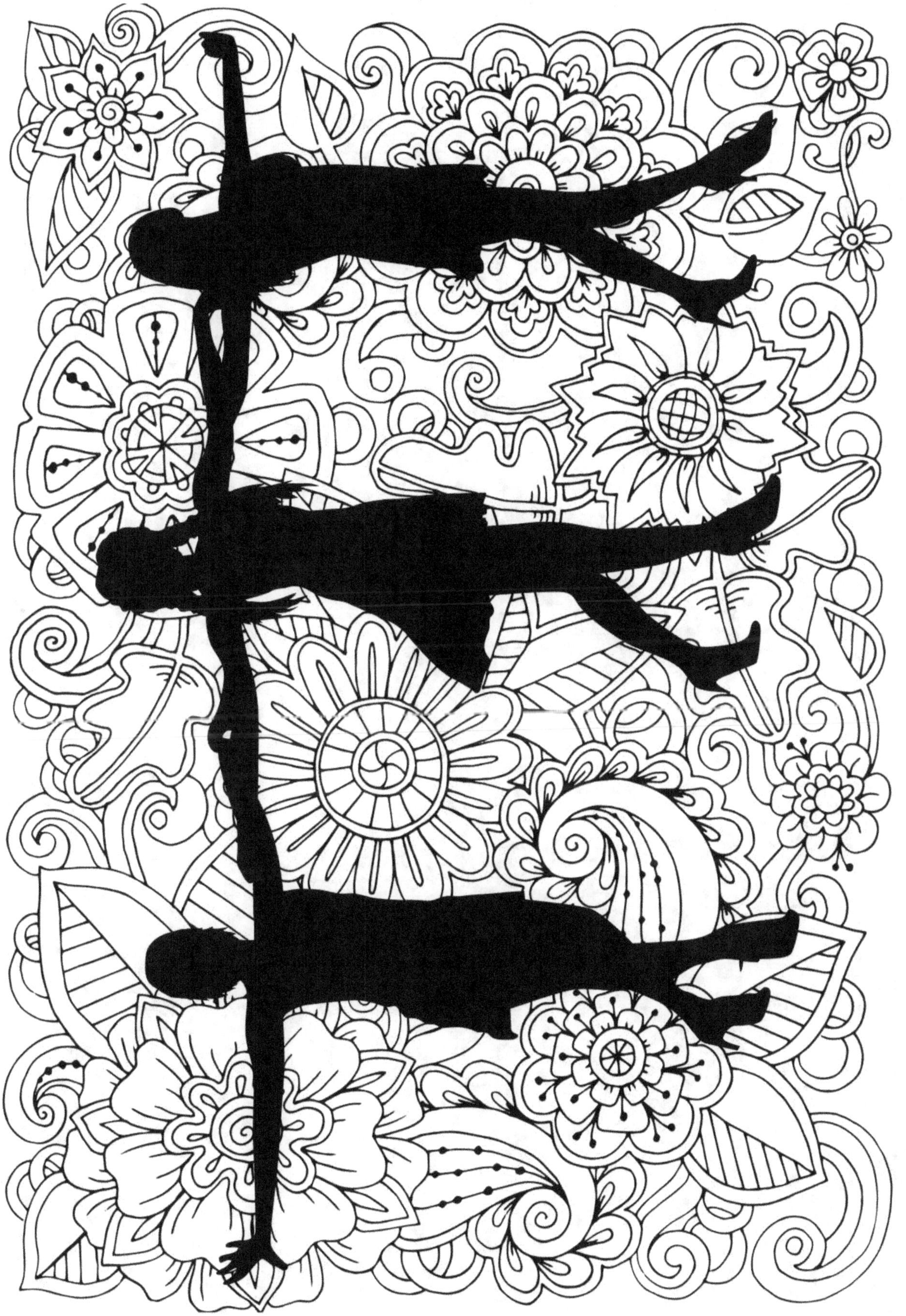

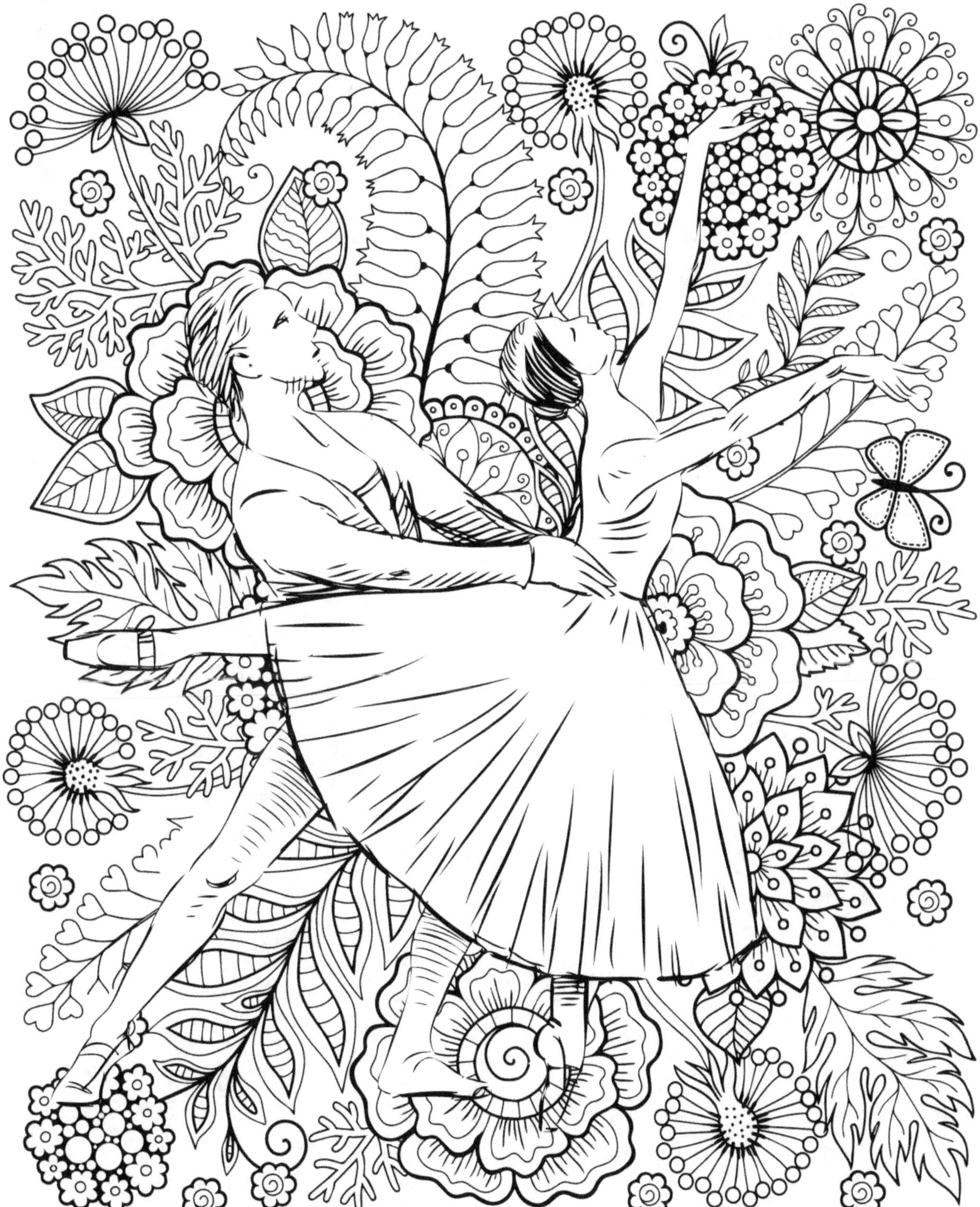

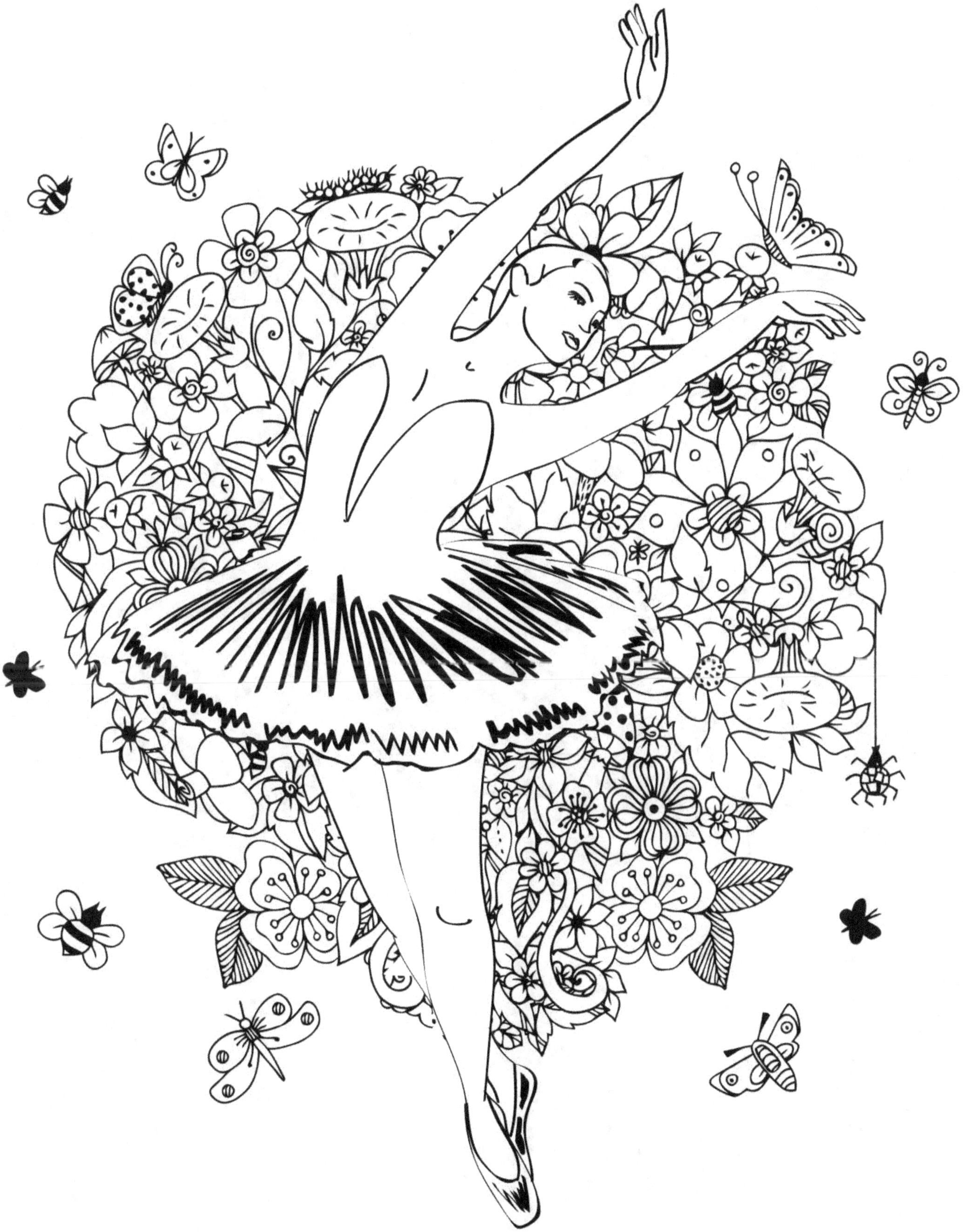

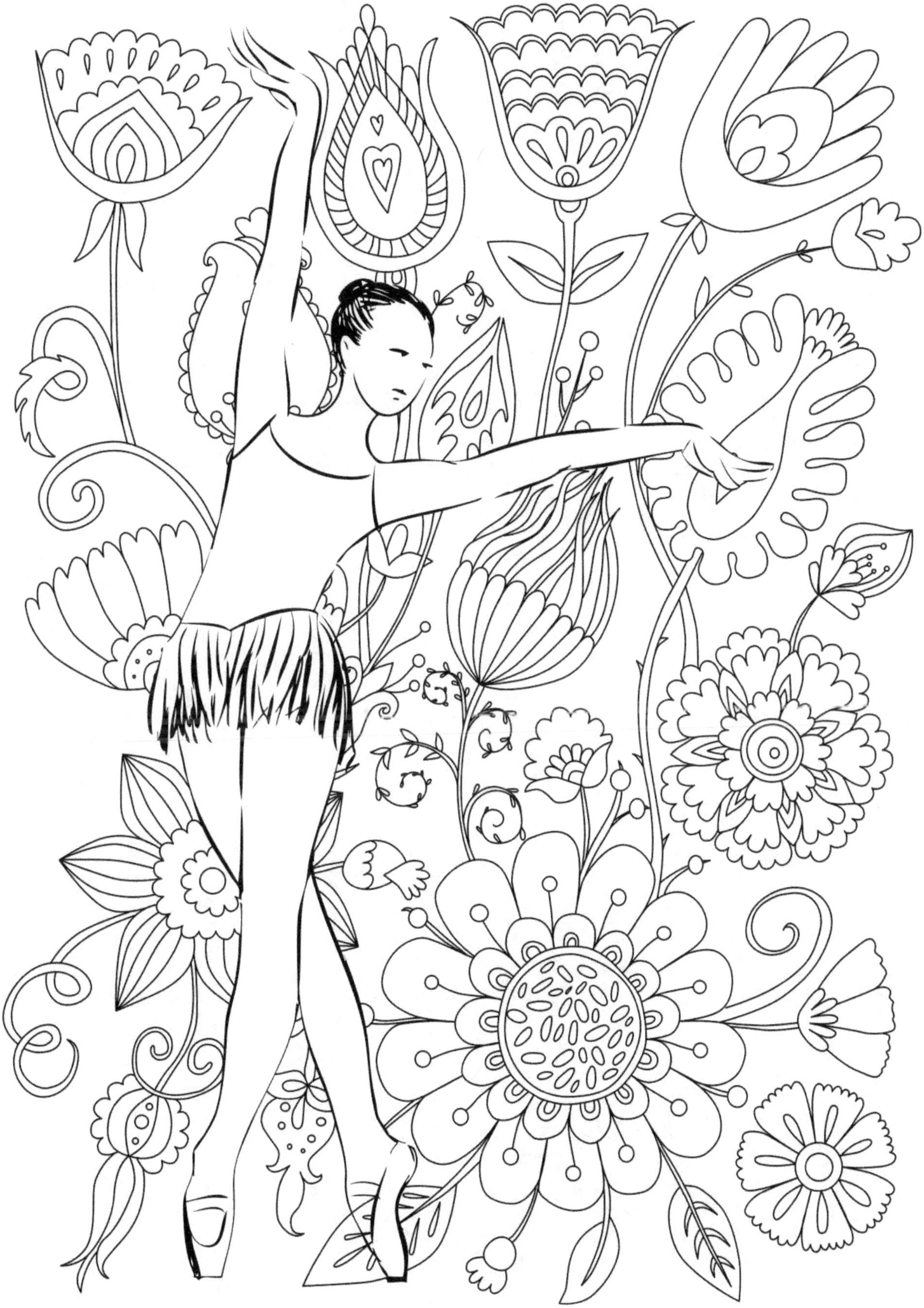

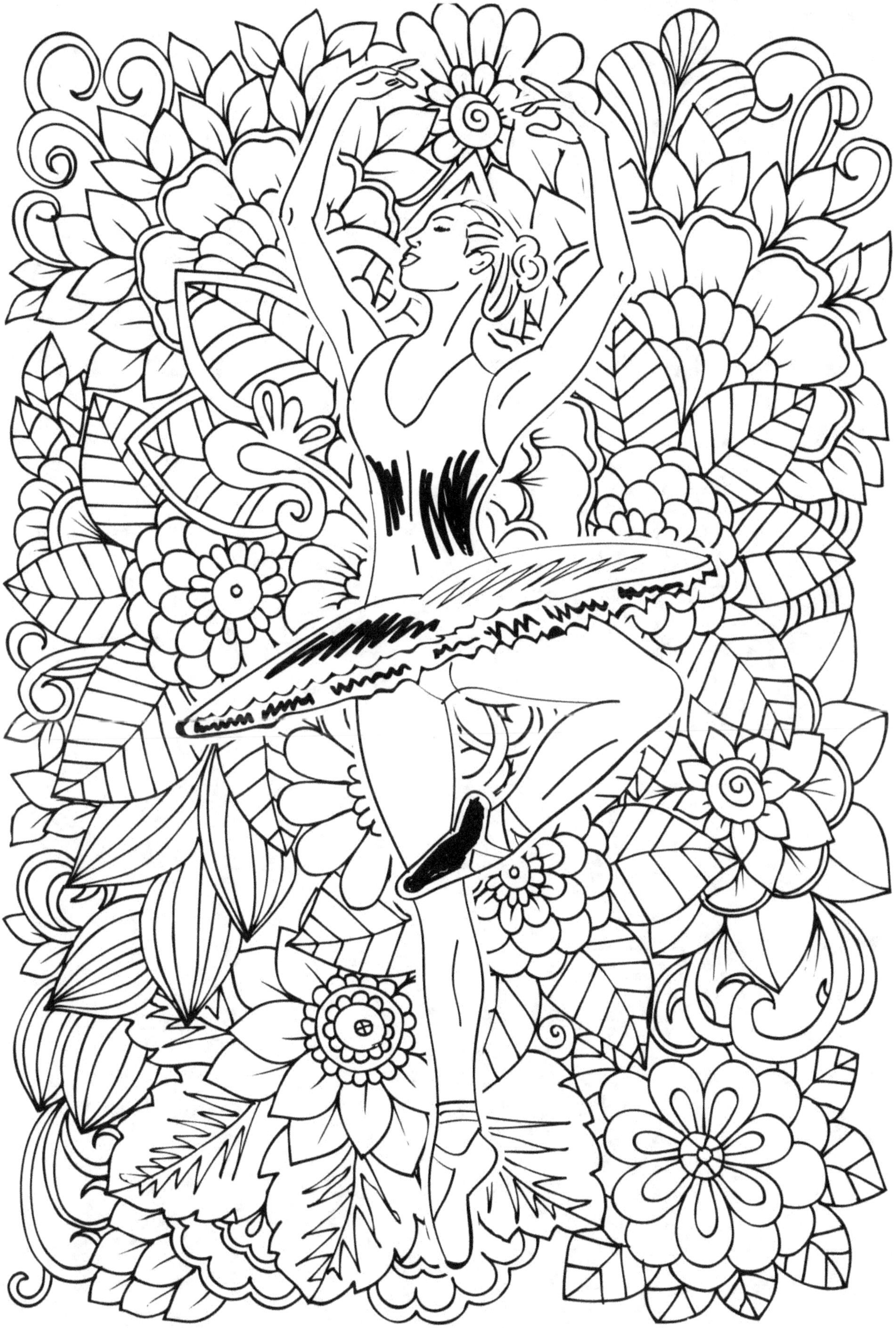

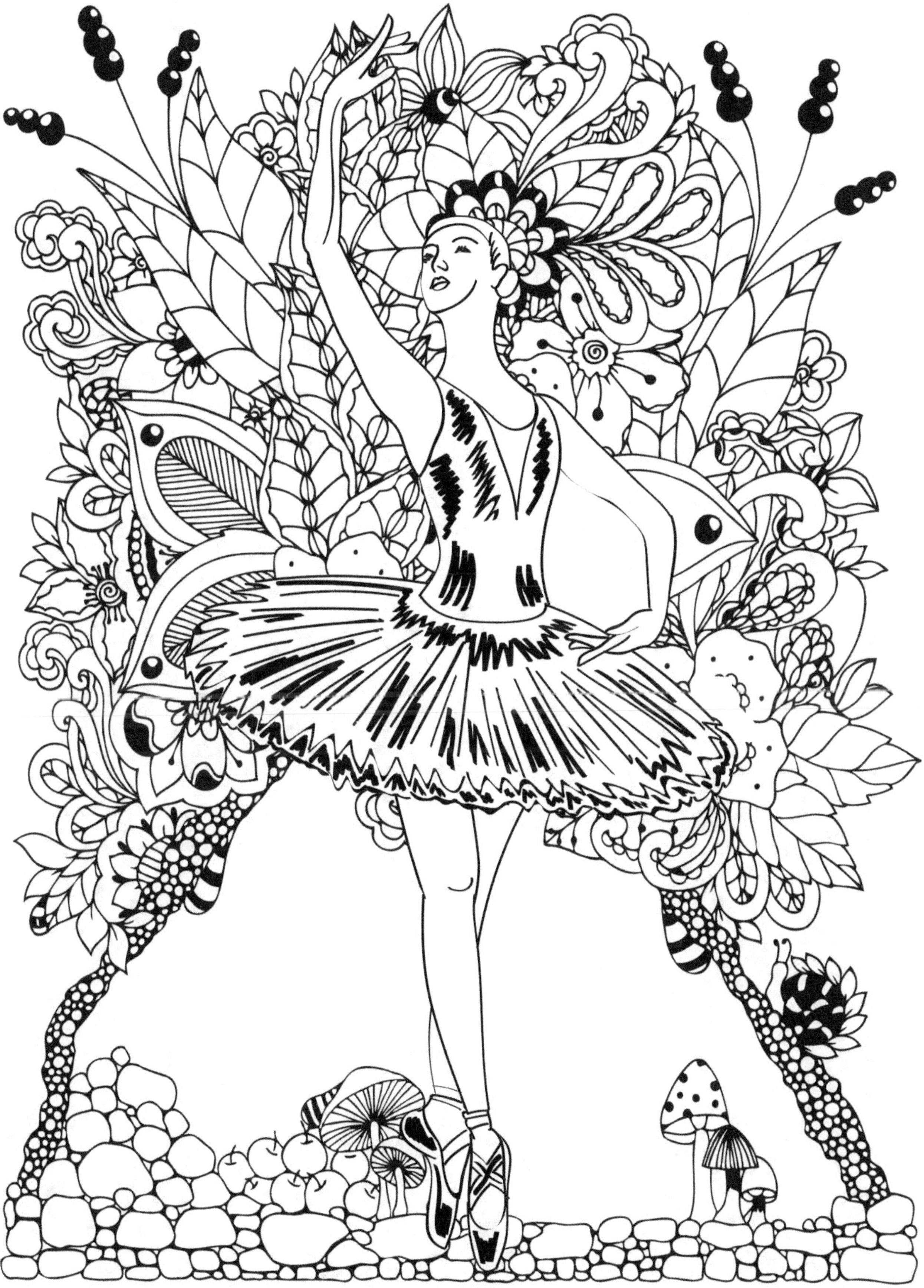

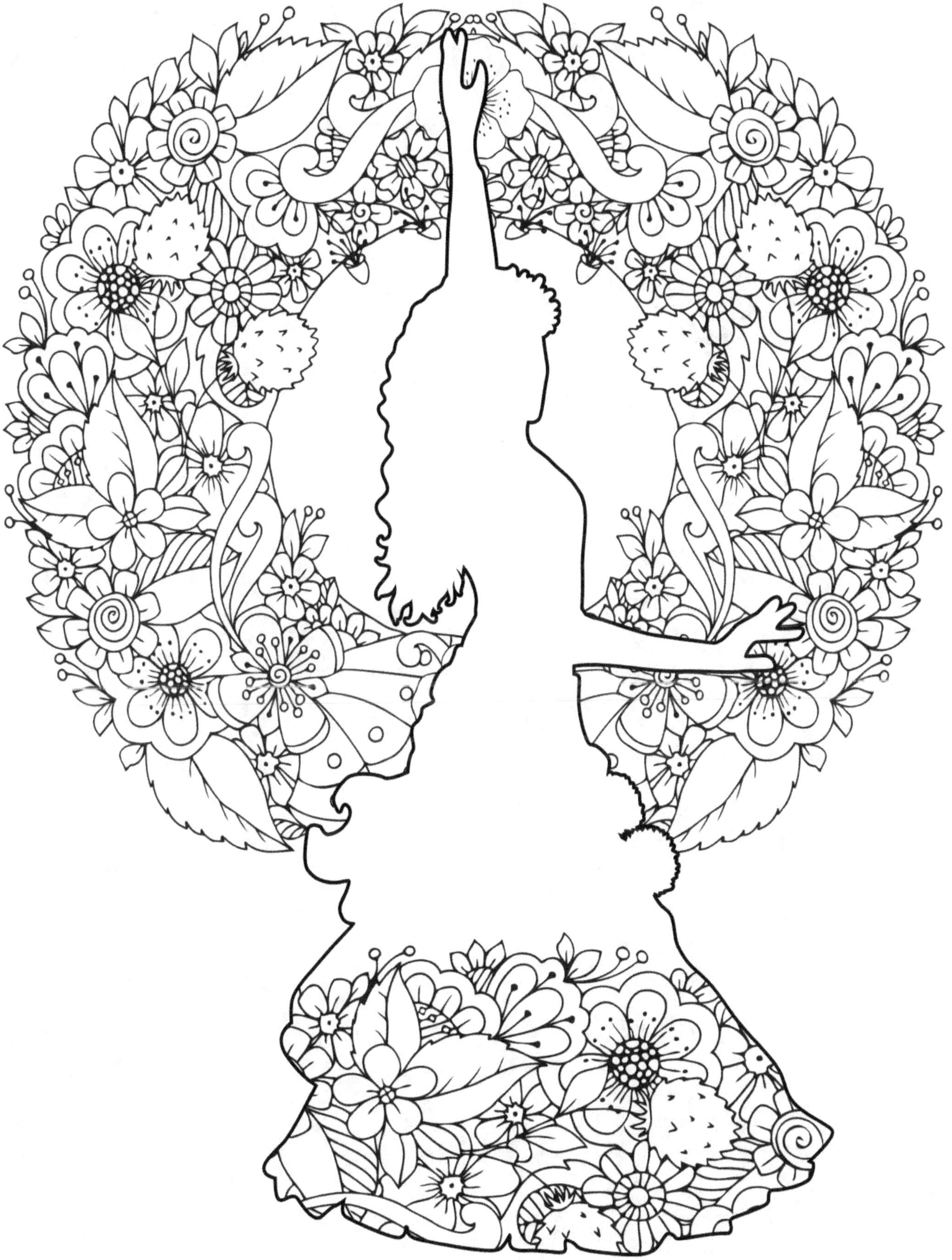

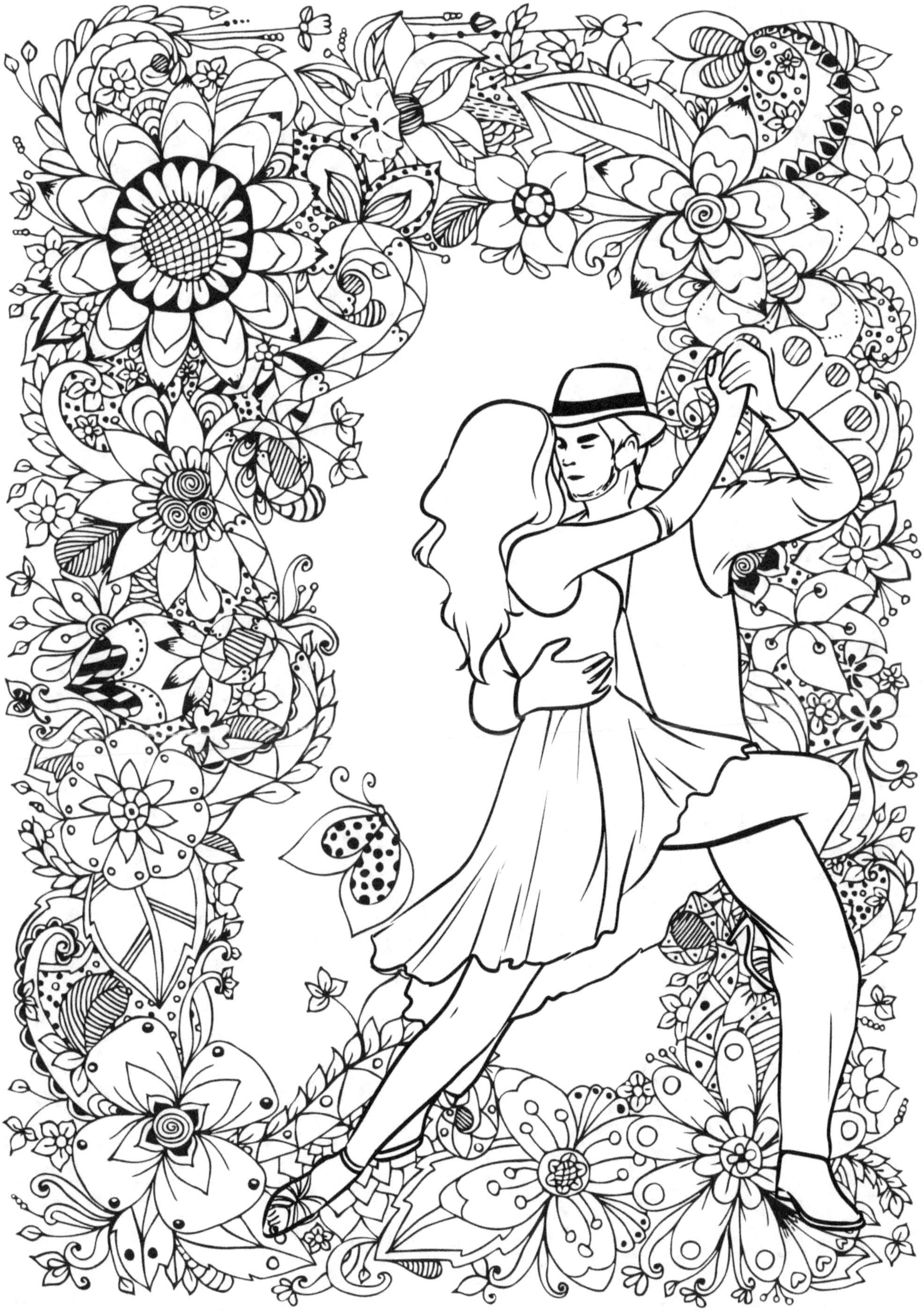

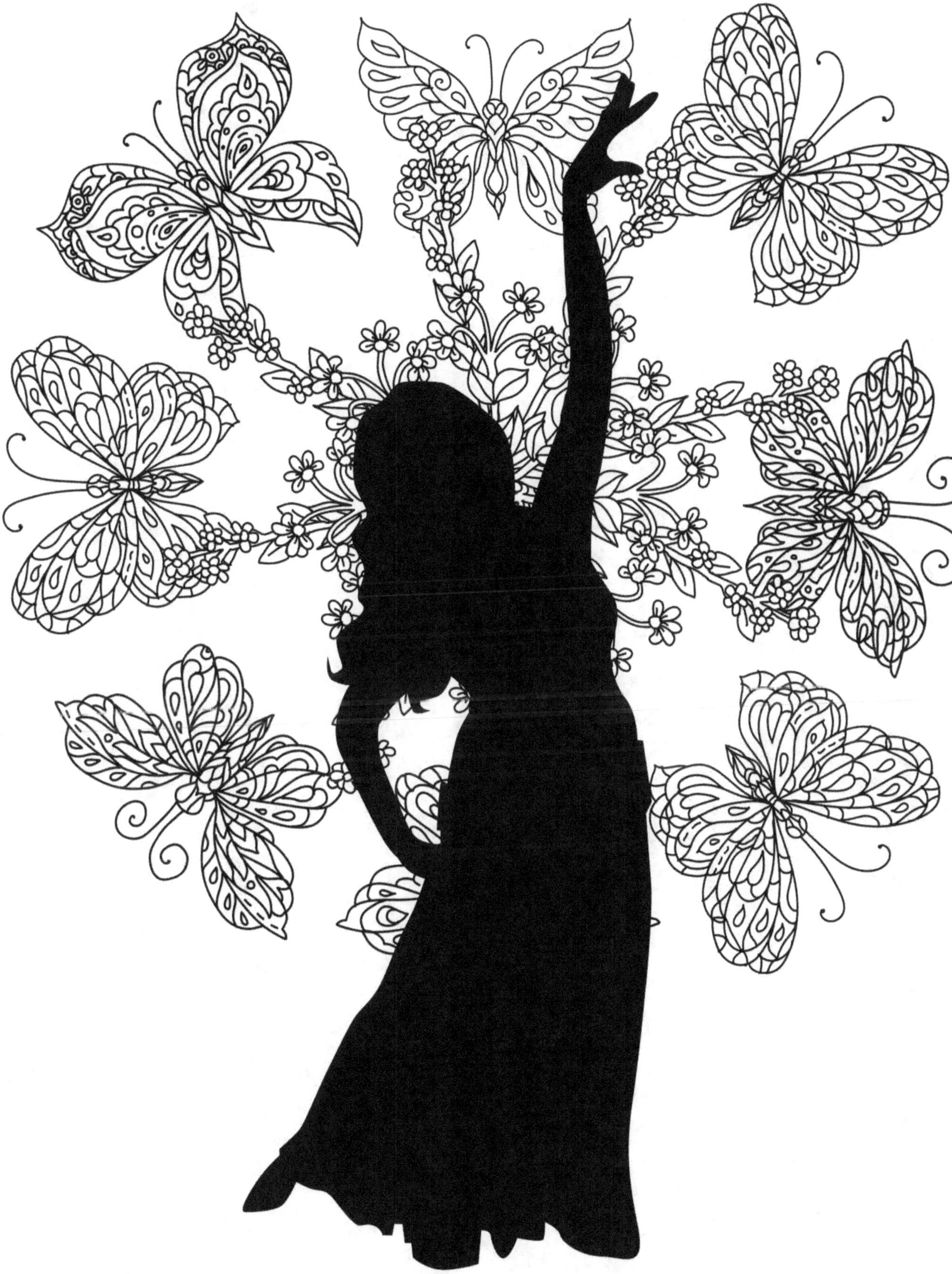

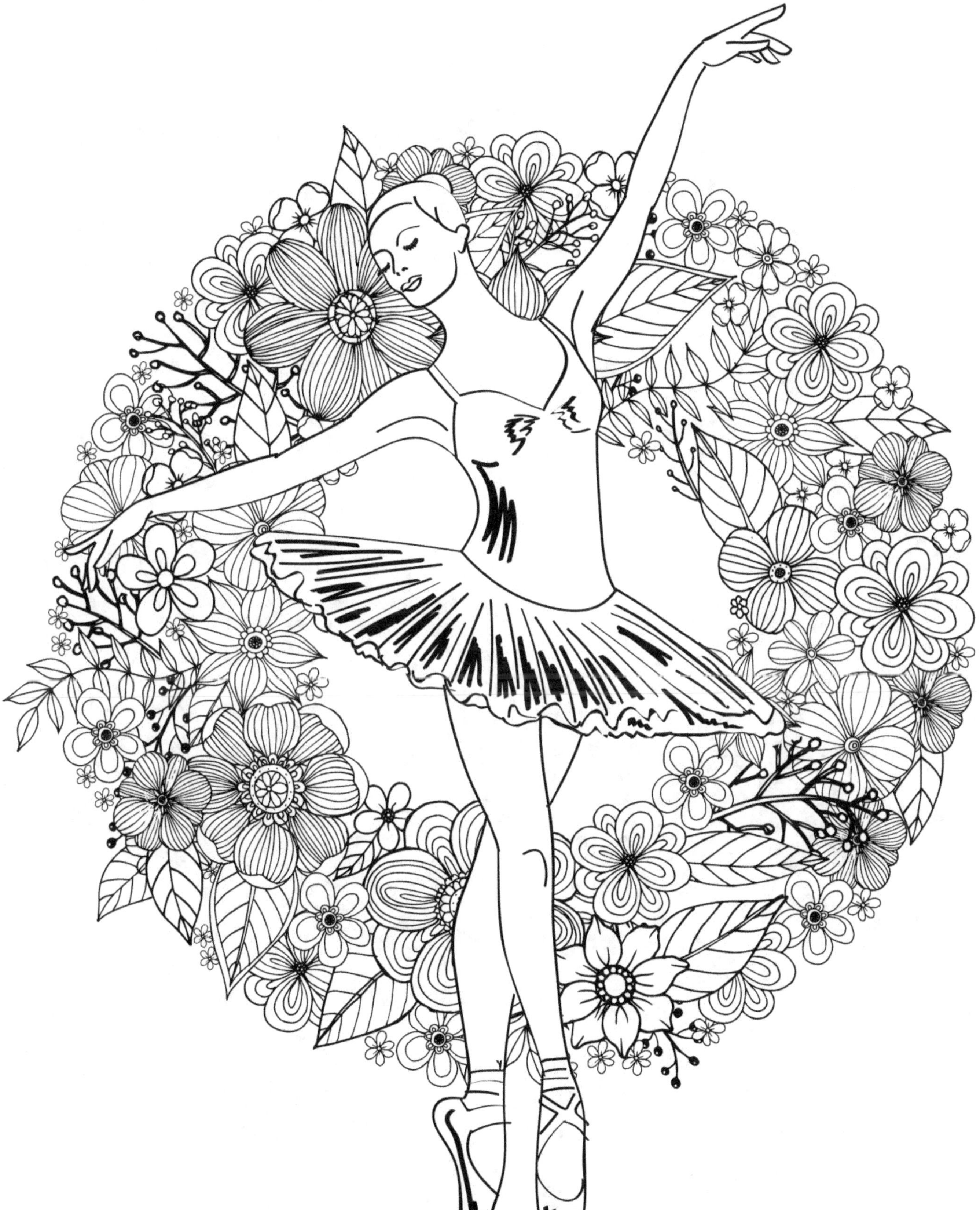

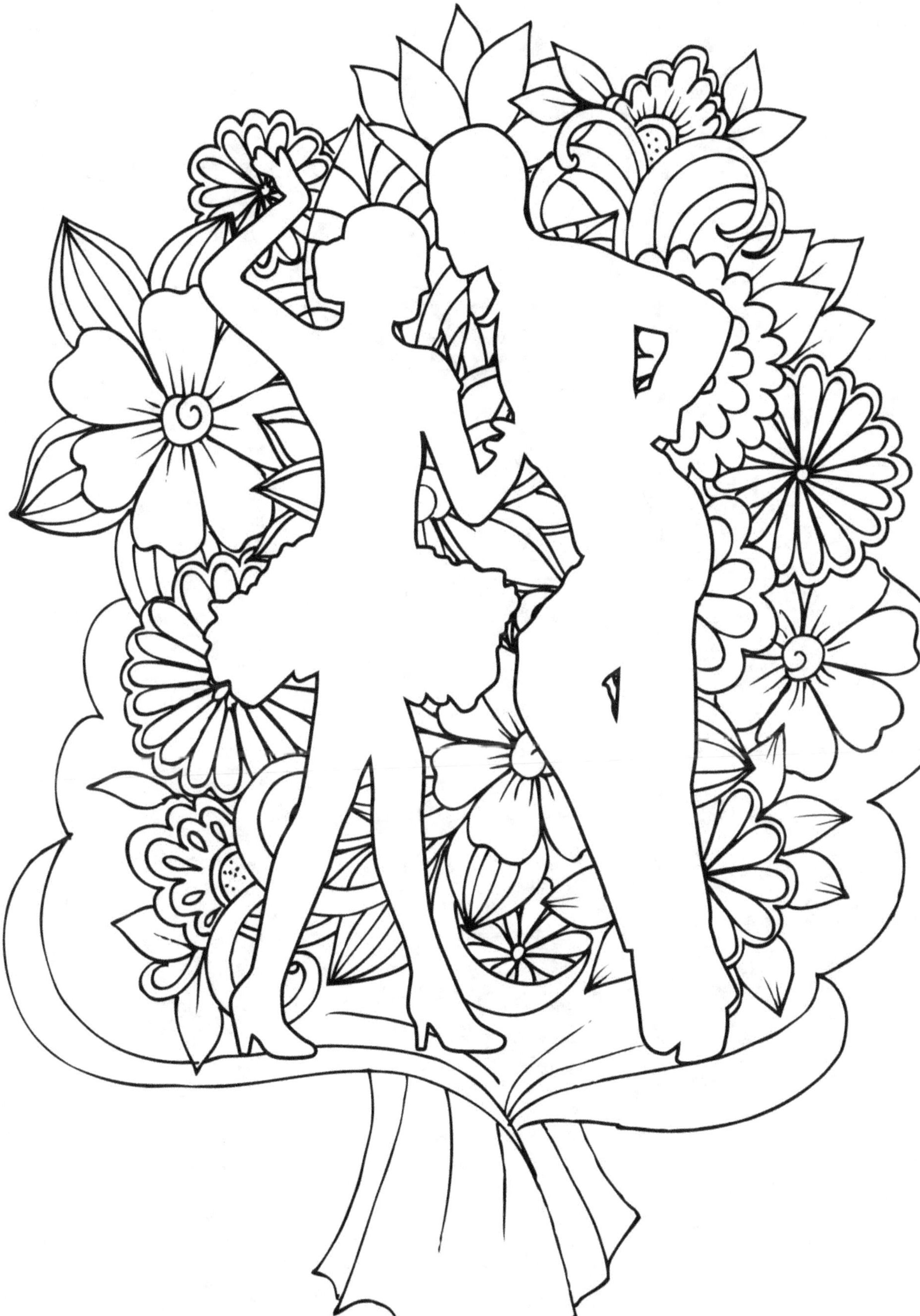

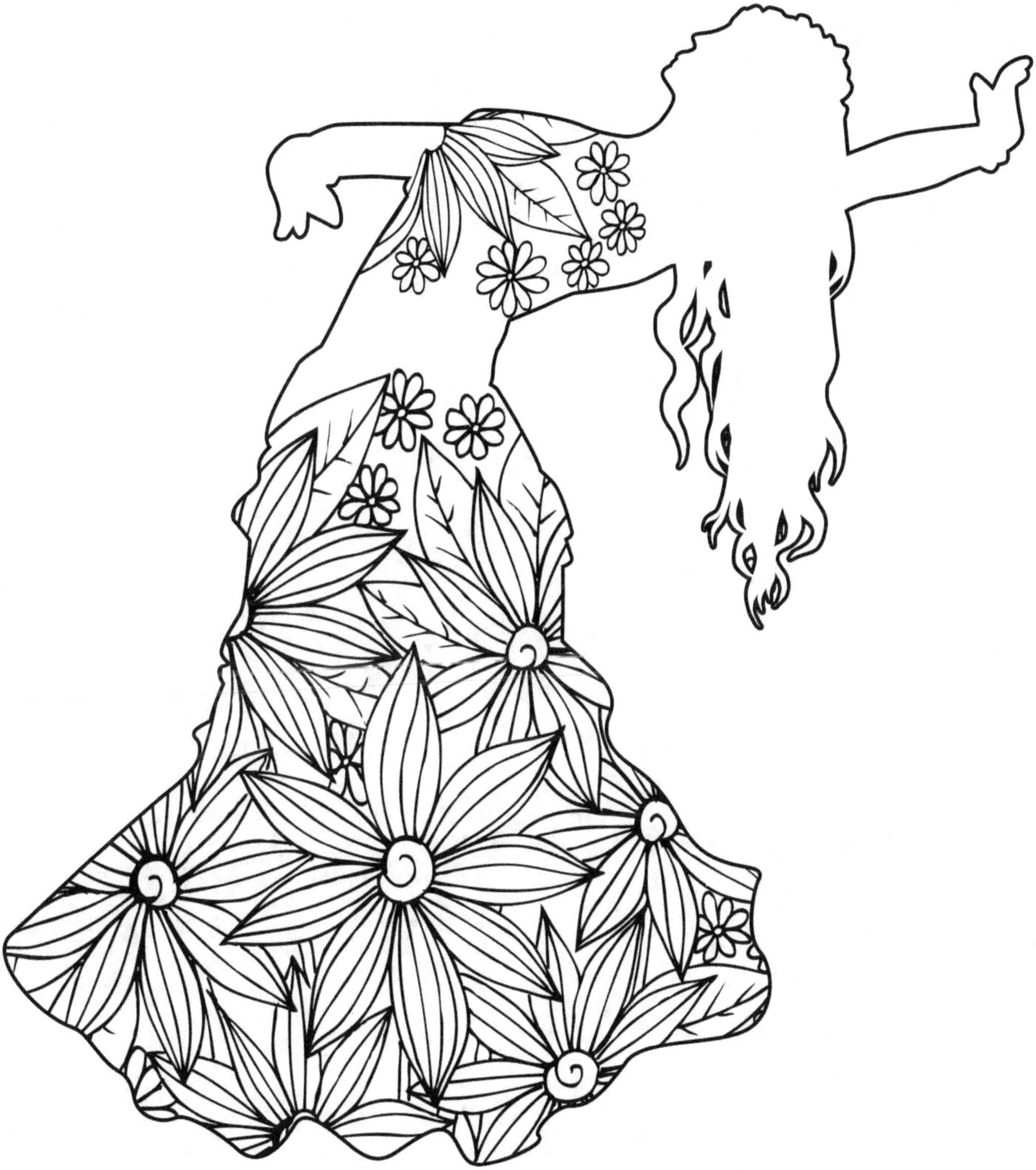

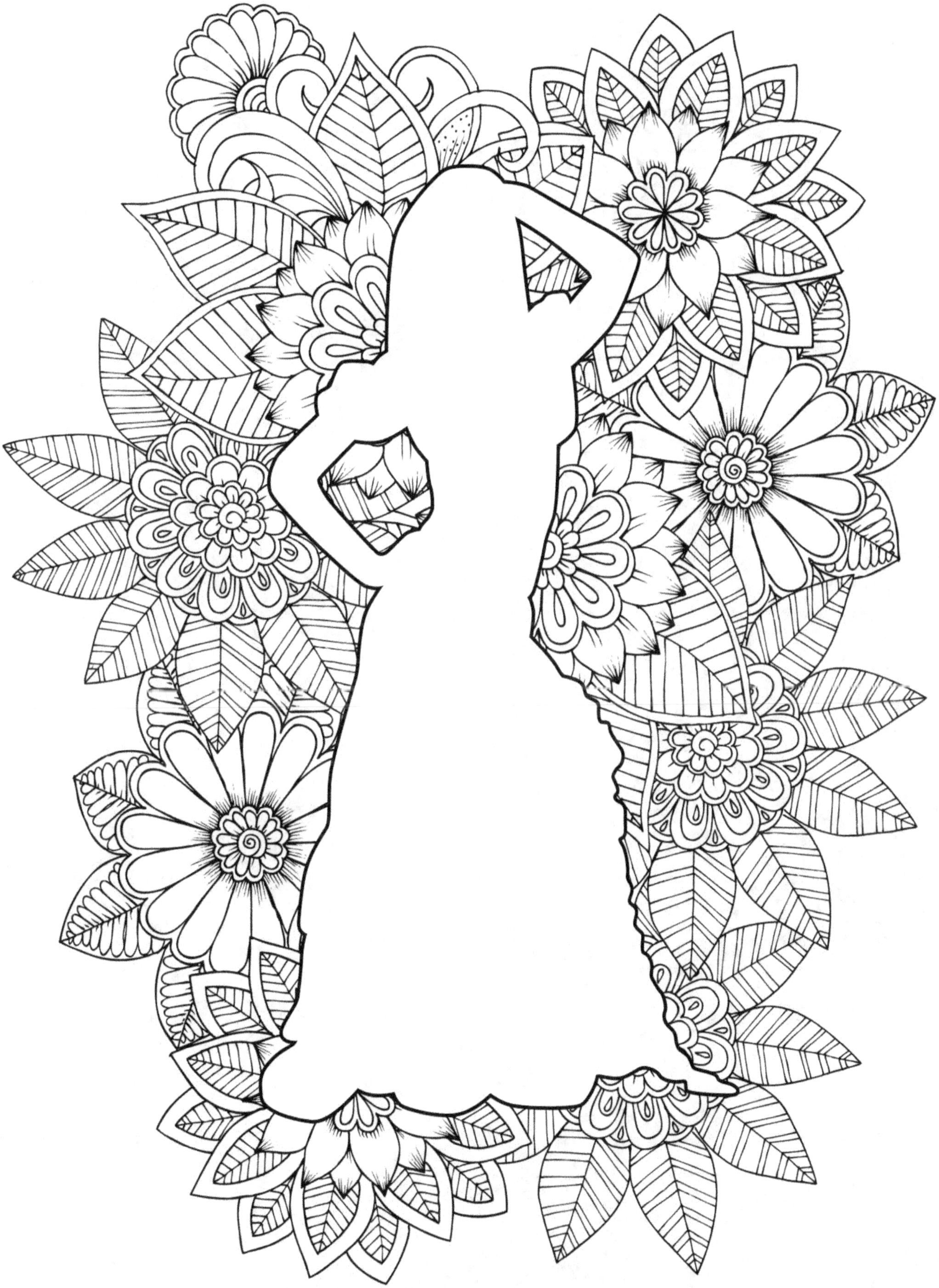

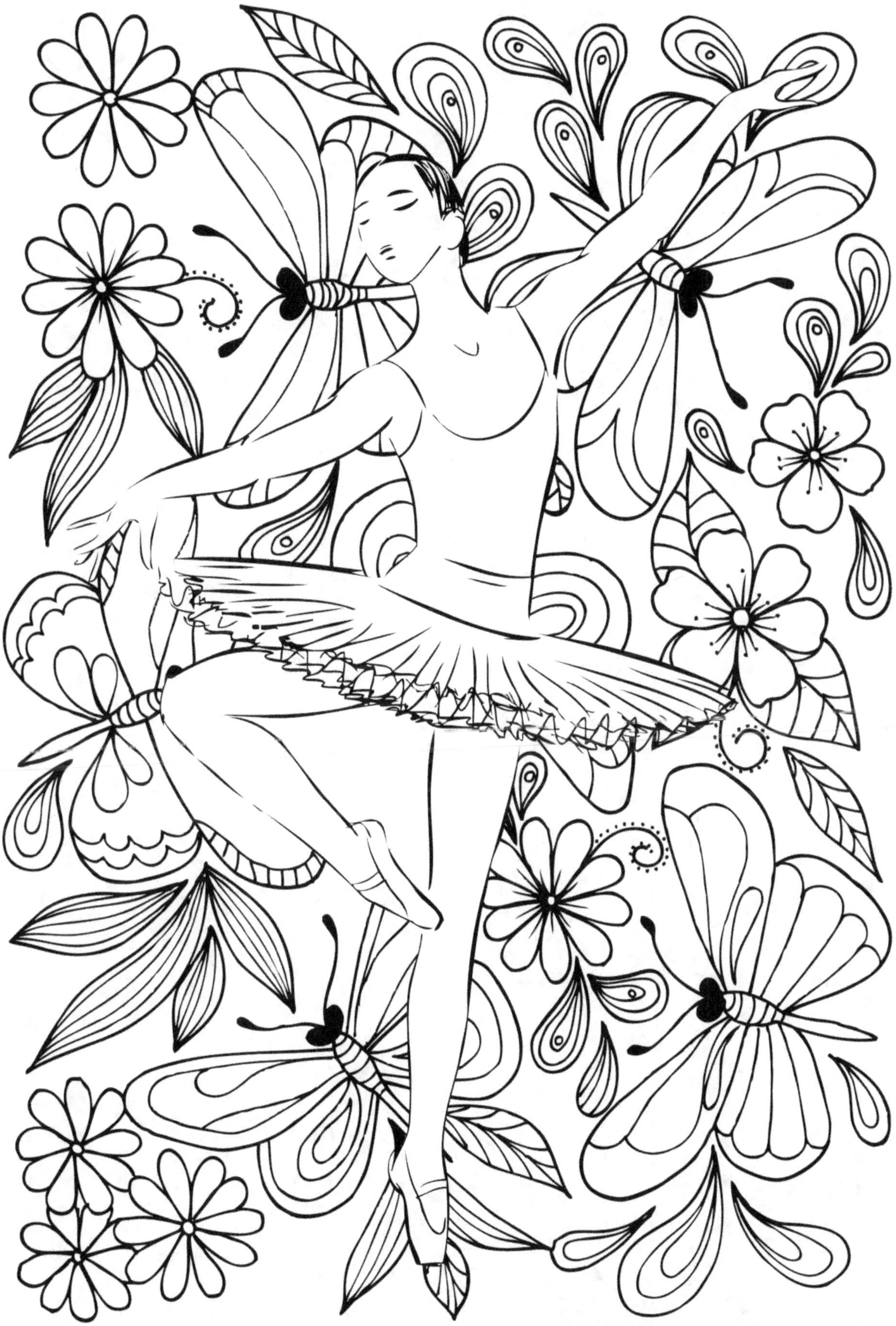

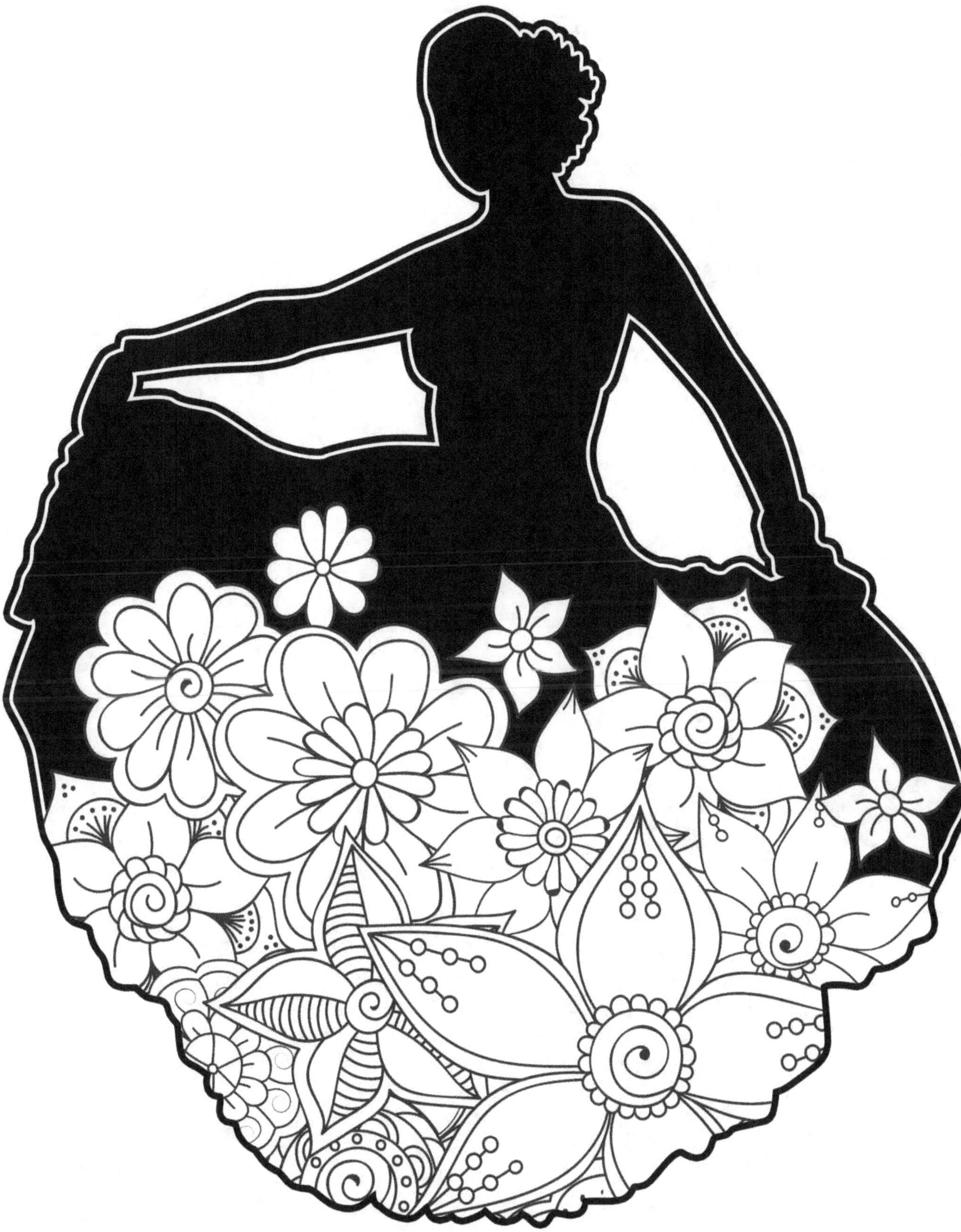

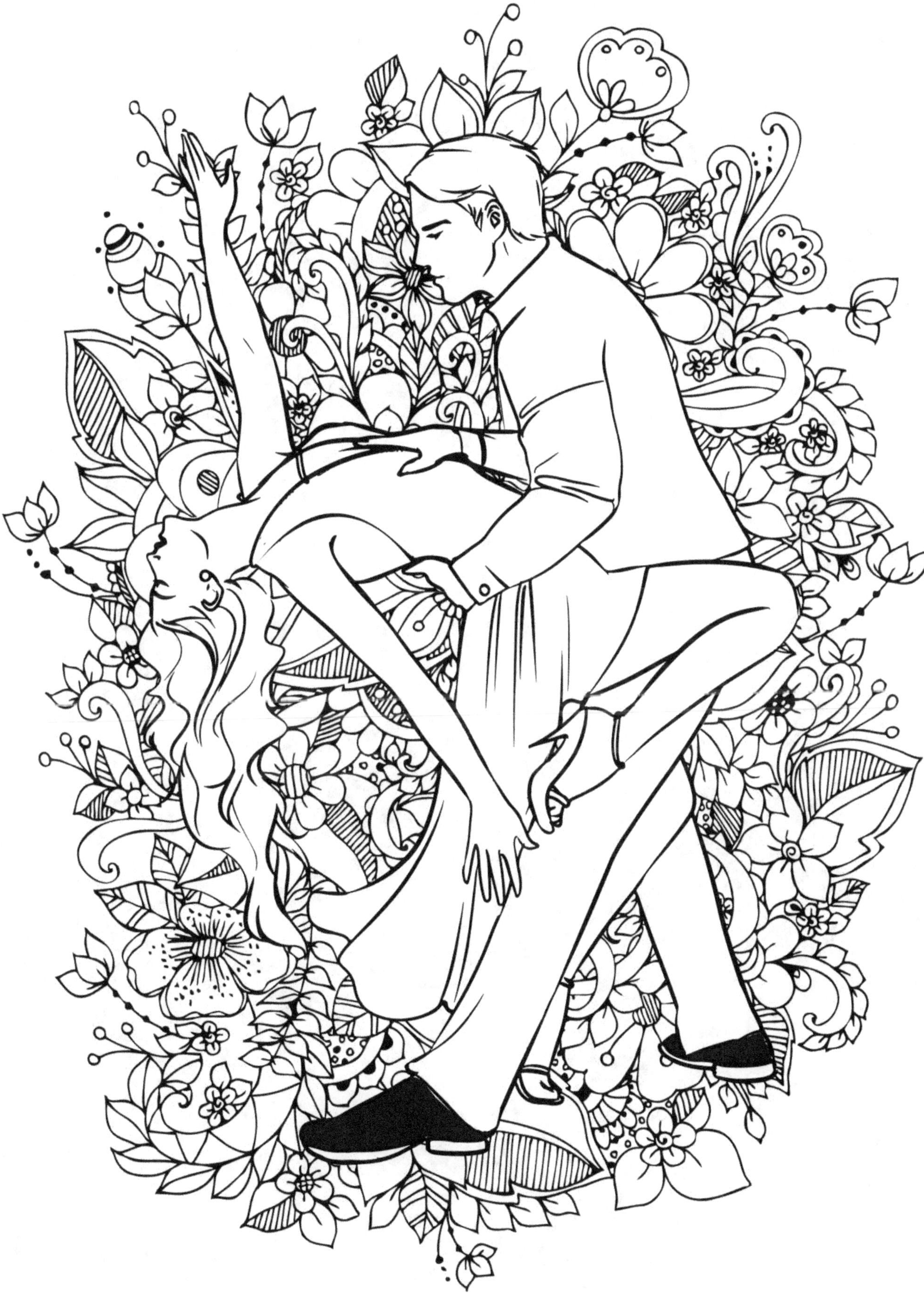

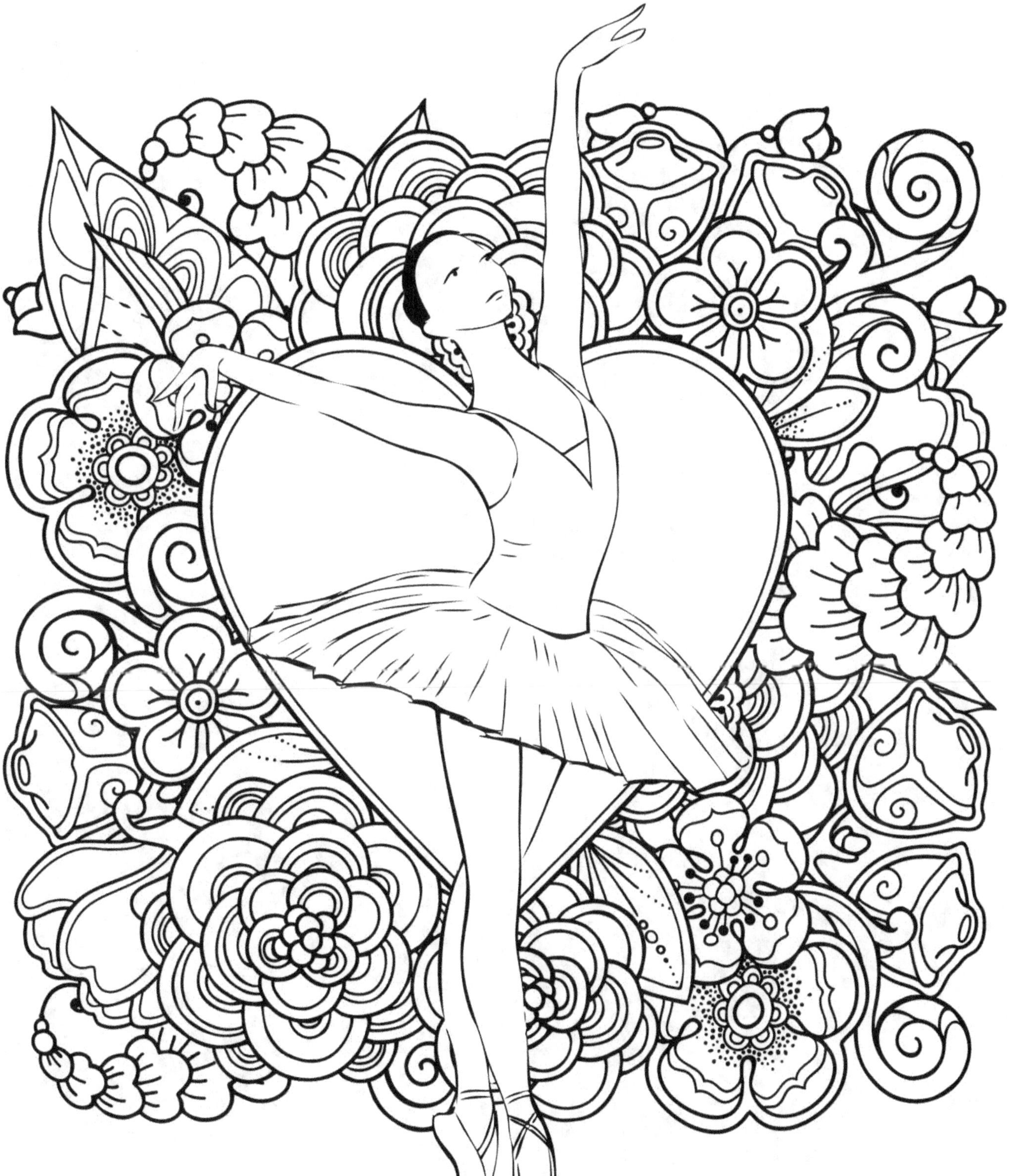

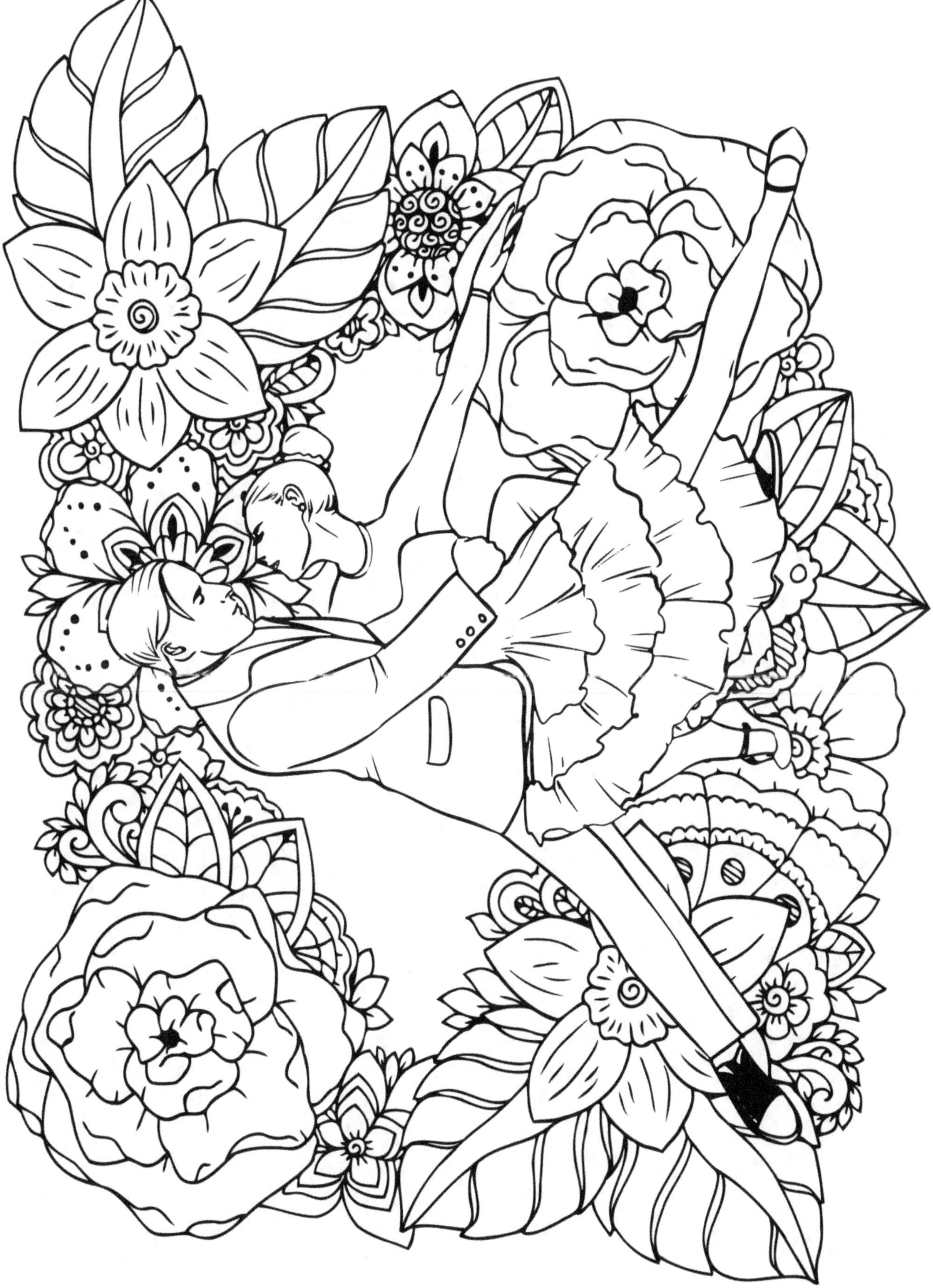

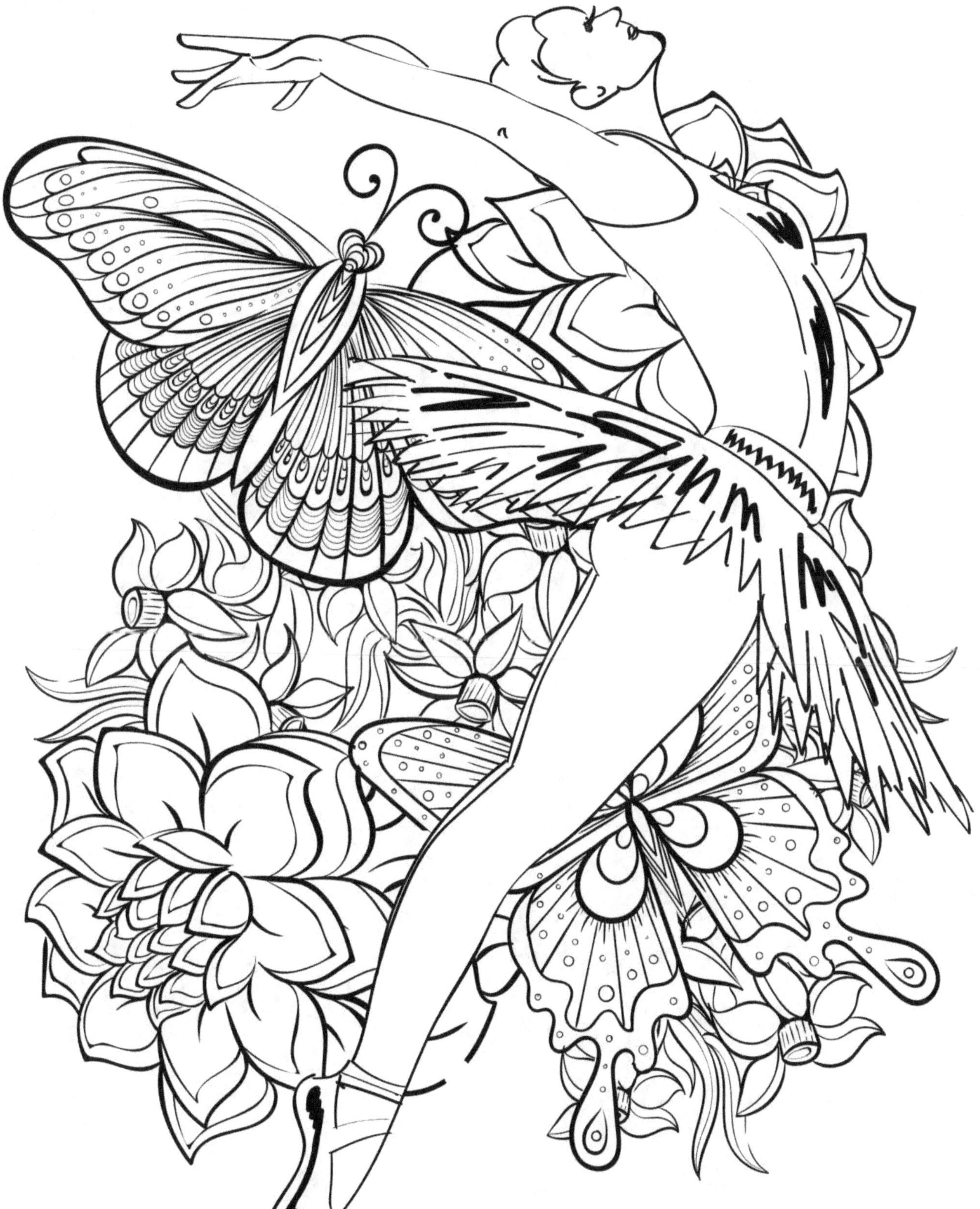

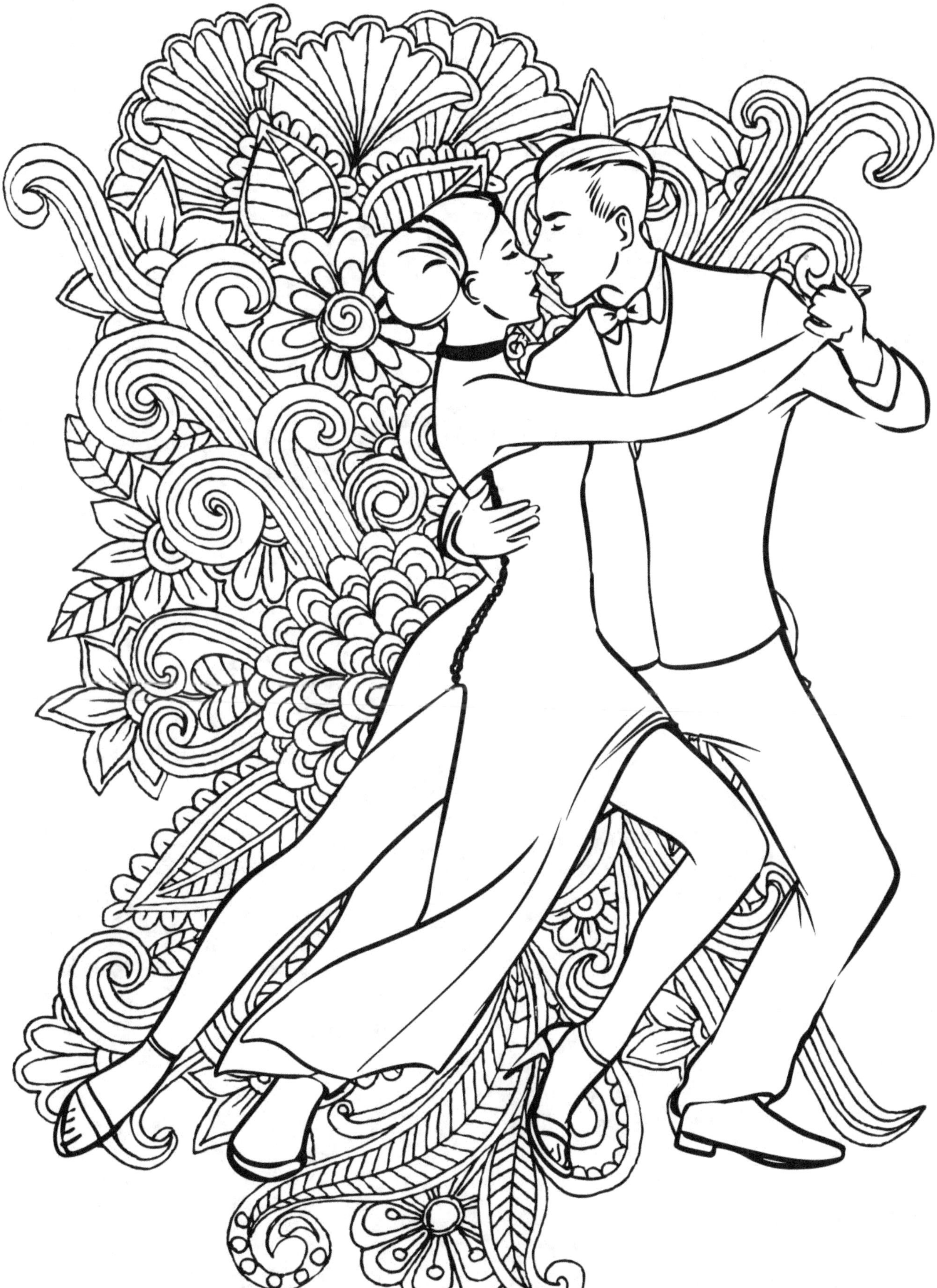

www.ingramcontent.com/pod-product-compliance
Lightning Source LLC
Chambersburg PA
CBHW081639220526
45468CB00009B/2497
* 9 7 8 1 9 7 4 4 9 6 8 3 9 *